Pebble™

First Biographies

Benjamin Banneker

by Eric Braun

Consulting Editor: Gail Saunders-Smith, PhD
Consultant: Steven X. Lee, Director
Benjamin Banneker Historical Park and Museum
Baltimore, Maryland

Capstone
press
Mankato, Minnesota

Pebble Books are published by Capstone Press,
151 Good Counsel Drive, P.O. Box 669, Mankato, Minnesota 56002.
www.capstonepress.com

1 2 3 4 5 6 10 09 08 07 06 05

Library of Congress Cataloging-in-Publication Data
Braun, Eric, 1971–
    Benjamin Banneker / by Eric Braun.
    p. cm.—(Pebble books. First biographies)
    Includes bibliographical references and index.
    ISBN 0-7368-4233-0 (hardcover)
    1. Banneker, Benjamin, 1731–1806. 2. Astronomers—United States—Biography—
Juvenile literature. 3. Scientists—United States—Biography—Juvenile literature.
4. African American scientists—Biography—Juvenile literature. I. Title. II. Series:
First biographies (Mankato, Minn.)
QB36.B22B73 2006
520'.92—dc22   2004029506

Summary: Simple text and photographs introduce the life of Benjamin Banneker, an
astronomer and mathematician, who wrote almanacs and helped survey the land for
the U.S. capital.

Note to Parents and Teachers

The First Biographies set supports national history standards for
units on people and culture. This book describes and illustrates the
life of Benjamin Banneker. The images support early readers in
understanding the text. The repetition of words and phrases helps
early readers learn new words. This book also introduces early
readers to subject-specific vocabulary words, which are defined in
the Glossary section. Early readers may need assistance to read
some words and to use the Table of Contents, Glossary, Read More,
Internet Sites, and Index sections of the book.

Table of Contents

Time Line

1731
born

Born Free

Benjamin Banneker was born in Maryland in 1731. At that time, most black people in America were slaves. But Benjamin was not a slave. His family owned a farm.

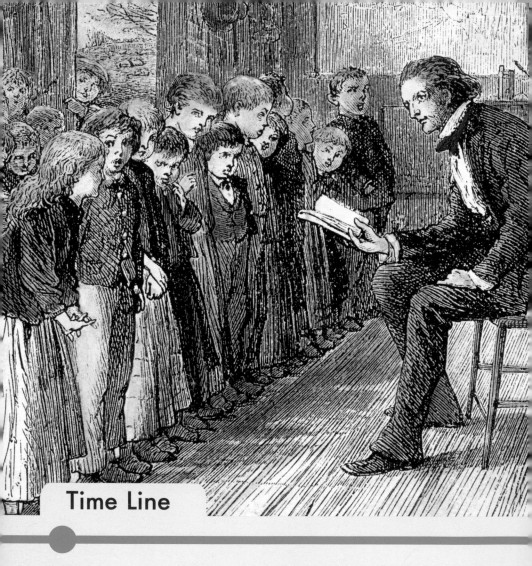

Time Line

1731
born

6

Benjamin's grandmother taught him to read. Benjamin was curious. He went to school to learn more. He learned to write. He studied math.

◀ a school like the one Benjamin attended

1731
born

1751–1753
builds wooden
clock

Benjamin's Studies

Benjamin was curious throughout his life. At age 20, he took apart a watch. Benjamin studied each tiny piece. He then carved his own clock.

a wood clock similar to the clock Benjamin built

Time Line

1731
born

1751–1753
builds wooden
clock

1788
begins to study
astronomy

At age 57, Benjamin began
to study astronomy. He read
books about the stars.
He used a telescope
to study the night sky.

two astronomers using a telescope to study the
night sky

Time Line

1731
born

1751–1753
builds wooden
clock

1788
begins to study
astronomy

Benjamin learned to survey land. He measured and planned how to use the land. In 1791, Benjamin helped survey the new capital of the United States.

1791
helps survey land
for U.S. capital

Time Line

1731
born

1751–1753
builds wooden
clock

1788
begins to study
astronomy

Benjamin wanted to share what he had learned from his studies. He wrote a book of facts called an almanac. At that time, few blacks had written books in America.

1791
helps survey land for U.S.
capital; publishes the first
of six almanacs

15

Time Line

1731
born

1751–1753
builds wooden
clock

1788
begins to study
astronomy

16

In Benjamin's time,
many white people thought
black people couldn't learn.
But Benjamin's studies proved
a black person could learn.

In the 1700s, most blacks were slaves who worked in fields.

1791
helps survey land for U.S. capital; publishes the first of six almanacs

Time Line

1731
born

1751–1753
builds wooden
clock

1788
begins to study
astronomy

Benjamin Speaks Out

Benjamin wrote a letter
to Thomas Jefferson.
He told Jefferson
that black people could learn
to read and write.
Jefferson thanked Benjamin
for his letter.

 Thomas Jefferson

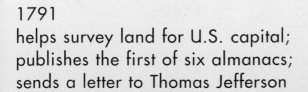

1791
helps survey land for U.S. capital;
publishes the first of six almanacs;
sends a letter to Thomas Jefferson

Benjamin Banneker

Black Heritage USA 15c

Time Line

1731	1751–1753	1788
born	builds wooden clock	begins to study astronomy

20

Benjamin showed that blacks could do as well as whites. They just needed a chance to learn. Benjamin died in 1806. He is still known for his work and almanacs.

◀ U.S. postage stamp honoring Benjamin

1791
helps survey land for U.S. capital;
publishes the first of six almanacs;
sends a letter to Thomas Jefferson

1806
dies

Glossary

almanac—a book based on astronomy published every year that has facts on many subjects, such as farming

astronomy—the science of space, stars, and planets

slave—a person owned by another person; slaves were not free to choose their homes or jobs.

survey—to measure land in order to make a plan for how to use it, such as laying out the streets of a new city

telescope—a tool that makes faraway objects look larger and closer

Thomas Jefferson—the third president of the United States; Jefferson was secretary of state when Benjamin wrote a letter to him.

Read More

Maupin, Melissa. *Benjamin Banneker.* Journey to Freedom. Chanhassen, Minn.: Child's World, 2000.

Zschock, Martha Day. *Journey Around Washington, D.C., from A to Z.* Beverly, Mass.: Commonwealth Editions, 2004.

Internet Sites

FactHound offers a safe, fun way to find Internet sites related to this book. All of the sites on FactHound have been researched by our staff.

Here's how:

1. Visit *www.facthound.com*

2. Type in this special code **0736842330** for age-appropriate sites. Or enter a search word related to this book for a more general search.

3. Click on the **Fetch It** button.

FactHound will fetch the best sites for you!

Index

Word Count: 231
Grades: 1–2
Early-Intervention Level: 20

Editorial Credits
Katy Kudela, editor; Heather Kindseth, set designer; Patrick D. Dentinger, book designer;
    Kelly Garvin, photo researcher/photo editor

Photo Credits
Archives Center, National Museum of American History, Behring Center, Smithsonian
Institution, 8; Getty Images Inc./Hulton Archive, 4, 18; The Granger Collection, New York,
1, 6, 14, 16, 20; Library of Congress, 10; Photographs and Prints Division, The Schomburg
Center for Research in Black Culture, The New York Public Library, Astor, Lenox and
Tilden Foundation, cover, 12